The Calling Heart

A Litany compiled by
Shaykh Fadhlalla Haeri

Zahra Publications

ISBN: 978-1-7764901-3-4

First Published in 2024 by Zahra Publications

Distributed and Published by Zahra Publications
PO Box 50764
Wierda Park, 0149
Centurion
South Africa
Email info@shaykhfadhlallahaeri.com
www.shaykhfadhlallahaeri.com
www.zahrapublications.pub

Set in 10 point in Lexicon

The Calling Heart

A Litany compiled by
Shaykh Fadhlalla Haeri

Zahra Publications

Supplication

In Arabic the word *nabi,* prophet, is from the root word which means news, view or insight. The word *rasul* is from the root word meaning message, letter, instruction or commands. Our Prophet Muhammad *(pbuh)* was both a prophet and a messenger. His message was based on unity and his news was based on the truth which leads to self-realization, to lasting inner contentment based on faith, fearful awareness, and the knowledge of Allah's perfect ways and designs. Muhammad's *(pbuh)* life, conduct and most perfect and natural ways were described as the 'Living Qur'an'.

Prophetic Traditions

The Prophetic teachings and practices are very rich regarding the importance of supplication and prayers to Allah and calling upon His Attributes and Beautiful Names. The Prophet *(pbuh)* recommended prayers and supplications for specific times and certain circumstances, which are described later in this chapter.

The Prophet (*pbuh*) has taught that:
- Supplication is itself worship.
- Supplication is the core of worship.
- Nothing will change one's destiny except supplication and prayers.
- Supplication from the slave to his Lord is one of his key duties and one of his greatest obligations.
- Supplication is the weapon of the believer; the foundation of religion and the light of the heavens and earth.

Supplication does not contradict the caller's state of contentment and inner ease. The blessed Prophet (*pbuh*) himself constantly called upon Allah, and encouraged repeating the supplication and persisting in prayer. He confirmed that Allah will deposit His gifts into the outstretched arms in prayer. He also discouraged people from asking of other human beings by saying that:

> *You repel people by asking them, whilst you draw closer to Allah by asking Him.*

This does not imply that one is not grateful for human kindness and consideration. The believer regards all creation as means and instruments of the Creator, under His control. To realize this truth, first accept it on trust and then you will witness its truth and be transformed through surrender (*islam*), faith (*iman*) and excellence *(ihsan)*. We need the Prophetic example perfection as a model to live by. Without loving the Prophet *(pbuh)* and believing in his just vicegerency *(Khilafah* of Allah) our progress will be faulty.

A useful paradigm is the hologram. If we groom the *nafs* on the model of the Prophetic conduct and *Din*, the hologram "I" is most prepared to be transformed by the truth, to be enlightened and witness the Light of The Supreme One – a small mirror reflecting the original Light of the Creator.

Etiquette of Du'a

Regarding the etiquette *(adab)* of *du'a* and calling Allah, the Prophet *(pbuh)* advised:

- Do not be hesitant or uncertain in your *du'a.*
- Do not be disappointed if your call is not answered by the time you expect it; it may be saved for you. 'Delay is not denial.'
- Repeat and persist in your calls, for he who knows Allah the most will ask Him for the most, and most frequently.
- Do not belittle the calls of others to Allah. He may answer the call of those you do not consider worthy of being answered.

As for unanswered calls we are told that the reason can include:

- The caller had not despaired from other people's help and was not truly in need or desperate, and thus not single-minded or focused in his calling upon Allah. Lack of sincerity and dependence on Allah is a big barrier.

- A call is not answered because the caller is not in *tawhid* and is not able to address or reach whom he is calling. This lack of deep courtesy will affect the appropriate transmission of the *dùa*.

- The caller has a very short-term need or desire and does not know what is really best for him in the longer term. Allah declares in the Qur'an (2:216):

  And it may be a good thing for you, but you detest it, and it may be wrong for you, and you desire it.

- The caller has not persisted enough in his calling, is impatient, or lacks certainty of the answer. He may also not be sure of, or clearin, what is needed.

The Beautiful Names and Attributes

Allah's most Beautiful Names have been endorsed in numerous books and compilations on the Prophetic tradition. One famous and popularly quoted Prophetic tradition of the Divine Names and Attributes is that:

'Allah has 99 Names and whoever counts them will enter the Garden.'

This tradition has often been quoted with slight variation by respected scholars, but essentially with the same meaning. These 99 Names are detailed in books by Tirmidhi, Ibn Majah, Hakim and others.

The Prophetic tradition does not restrict Allah's Names and Attributes to 99, but its emphasis is on counting, reciting, understanding, and recalling these Names. The Arabic word in this tradition is translated as 'counting' which also means to learn, memorize, reflect upon and gather (the meaning and connotation of these Names). Some commentators even highlight the need to apply the Name or Attribute to oneself, live by it, and visualize it so as to get closer to its deep meaning and implication for conduct.

The Prophet (*pbuh*) has said:

No one will ever be grieved if he asks Allah by every Name that belongs to Him, that He has called Himself by, or has brought down in His book, or has taught to any of His creation.

This means that Allah's Names and Attributes are far greater in power than we know or can relate to.

Best Times for Supplication

Every aspect in life undergoes dual cycles which connect, such as ebbing and flowing, expansion and contraction, rising and falling, living and dying. The season to plant is spring, when growth and expansion are most conducive naturally. In winter most plants contract and stop growing. As every action has a favorable time; so too does supplication, the timing of which relates to the state of the caller as well as the circumstances. Also there are naturally occurring periods during the year when planetary positions, electromagnetic fields, and other conditions, are most favorable.

The following is a brief list of favorable 'calendar' times for supplication:

- The Night of Power or Determination (*Laylat al-Qadr*), during the Fasting month of Ramadan
- The Day of *ʿArafat* of the *Hajj* (Pilgrimage)
- The Month of Ramadan
- Any Thursday Night
- Any Friday, during the day
- The middle of the night
- Before dawn (*fajr*)
- The last third of the night
- When the prayer (*salat*) is called – the short

interval between the call to prayer *(adhan)* and beginning the prayer

- Immediately after the prayer *(salat)*
- During prostration *(sajdah)*
- During a gathering for the remembrance of God *(dhikr)*
- During a rainstorm and other unusual earthly events such as earthquakes or tornadoes
- At the time of death of a believer *(mu'min)*
- At the time of birth
- And other occasions of special or personal significance

The Prophet *(pbuh)* has said that:

Three supplications will be clearly answered: At the time when a person is breaking his fast, when a pious and just spiritual leader (imam) makes supplication, and when an unjustly treated person calls out to Allah for help.

Ultimately the condition and state of the caller dictates the appropriate time to call. A pure heart, a clear and dedicated disposition, a sincere and desperate need, and high expectation of Allah, fear of Him and unconditional love and trust in Him all indicate a favorable 'time'.

The Prophet *(pbuh)* also said:
No people sit to remember Allah unless the angels encompass them, and the All-Merciful surrounds them, and peace descends upon them, and Allah will remember them.

Special Places

No doubt physical locations and places have their special influence, energy field and chemistry, which affect the power and efficiency of calling and, therefore, the result and effect. On places that have special merit the Prophet *(pbuh)* said, *'Supplications are acceptable when made at the side of the Kabah, the House of God in Makkah.'* There is also great merit in supplication made in the *Masjid Al-Haram* in Makkah and the Mosque of the Prophet *(pbuh)* in Madinah. Also the Prophet *(pbuh)* has said *'There is great merit in worshiping inside Allah's house, at Zamzam and Safa and Marwa and behind Maqam Ibrahim, Àrafat, Muzdalifah, Mina and at the three places where the stoning is done.'* All of those sites are in Makkah or nearby and are stages of the pilgrimage.

There are, of course, many other places on earth that help to increase the power of calling and enhance the state of the caller. Jerusalem, special shrines and places of lesser pilgrimage, and special mosques are among them. Places where prophets, *imams* and enlightened beings are buried also have a special influence in helping the caller to be better attuned, prepared, focused and in a humble and pleading mode.

When Supplication is Answered

Allah says in the Qur'an (2:186):
I will certainly answer the desperate when he calls.

The Prophet *(pbuh)* has said that:
He who has been treated unjustly will be answered even though an unbeliever.
The prayers of a father for his offspring will be answered, prayers of a just spiritual leader (imam), prayers of a virtuous man, of a virtuous son, the prayers of the traveler, and for a Muslim brother or sister when not present.
The fastest supplication to be answered is the calling of a stranger for a stranger.

He who is calling knows his own state of serious need, desperation and urgency. He also knows the extent of his exclusive reliance on Allah. Among the signs that a supplication will be answered is the degree of faith, fearful awareness, a humble heart, weeping and a sense of last resort and desperation. It is also a good sign when the caller feels a relief and lightness as a result of supplication and prayer to Allah.

The Prophet (*pbuh*) has said:

Actions are as good as their final outcome. Do not judge a person until you see how he seals his action, for it can be that a person acts virtuously only a short time before his death and that causes him to enter the Garden.

Also a person can act evil and die upon this action and that will be the cause for him being in the Fire.

If Allah intends well for His slave He will put him to act virtuously before his death. Thus actions are as good as their final outcome.

Ultimately victory for a believer comes when he is constantly aware of his self and its limitations and weaknesses, and thus recognizes Allah's glorious generosity and ever-present mercy which cover and overcome human frailty and needs. The knowledge of Allah is the key to success in worship and in living one's religion, in preparation for the departure from this world of uncertainty and change, and for the return to the eternal Garden of bliss and its perfection.

Calling

To call upon Allah in times of need and to remember Allah in times of ease are part of the religion of Islam and the cornerstone of worship.

Allah says in the Qur'an (65:2-3):

And whosoever is in taqwa of Allah, He will give him a way out, and will provide for him from where he does not expect it.

And He provides for him from (sources) he never could imagine.

If anyone puts his trust in Allah, sufficient is Allah for him. For Allah will surely accomplish His purpose.

Verily, for all things has Allah appointed a due proportion (measure).

Thus cautious awareness, trust, and reliance upon Allah are the foundation of successful supplication and calling.

Prayers and supplications are motivated by various desires or needs and there are numerous types or levels of calling. One category is to do with unity, praise, and celebration, such as "Oh Lord to you belongs the Praise" (*Rabbana laka'l-hamd*). A second type is asking for forgiveness and the covering of faults and evil actions, such as, "Oh Allah forgive me" (*Allahumma ighfirli*), and "I seek forgiveness of Allah" (*Astaghfirullah*). Asking for forgiveness is actually asking Allah to 'cover' faults and shortcomings. Returning to the path is conditional upon regret for wrongdoing combined with the determination and commitment to not repeat the same error. A third type, which is the most prevalent, is asking Allah for a removal of an affliction or to bring about the fulfillment of a desire or need, such as, "Oh Allah bring me healing" (*Allahumma ishfini*), or, "Oh Allah provide for me" (*Allahumma ishfini*), or "Oh Allah give me help or victory" (*Allahumma unsurni*).

The courtesy of calling begins with real need and true reliance on Allah exclusively. He is the source and power behind all existence, experience and states.

Allah has revealed to the Prophet (*pbuh*),

I am as good as My slave's expectation of Me.

Expect therefore to be fully answered in the way that Allah knows best and according to His time and grace.

We must also remember what Allah says in the Qur'an:

...You may dislike a thing which is good for you and you may love a thing that is harmful for you. But Allah knows and you know not.

(2:216)

Courtesies of Supplication

The courtesies of the caller include physical cleanliness, to be ritually pure, to face the direction of prayer (*qiblah*), to lift one's hands, to start by saying, "In the Name of Allah," (*bismillah*), to praise the Prophet *(pbuh)*, and to have the mind focused upon Allah, His greatness, generosity and mercy. To have one's heart present, humbly, but in high anticipation and positiveness.

Every situation has its special supplication: e.g. before eating, whilst eating, after eating, when waking up, before sleeping, before leaving the house, before entering the bathroom and so on.

The Prophet *(pbuh)* has said:

He who has needs, let him be on good ablution (wudu'), and pray two cycles, and then praise Allah and send blessings upon the Prophet (pbuh) and his family,
and then make his supplication.

It is most important to be in certainty that Allah hears and that He will answer, yet repeatedly call often, and relentlessly.

As already mentioned, it is important to choose the appropriate time for supplication, as well as places that are conducive. The fasting month of Ramadan and the Night of Power, the month of Sha'ban, the first ten days of the month of Muharram *('Ashura')* and many other days are known to have special qualities. Pre-dawn supplication, before breaking fast, and in the afternoon are preferred times. As for places, Makkah,

Madinah, and numerous holy sites have greater benefits.

Allah says (39:53):

O My servants who have transgressed against their souls! Despair not of the Mercy of Allah, for Allah forgives all sins; for He is Often Forgiving, Most Merciful.

The Prophet (*pbuh*) has said:

Allah answers the call of a sincere Muslim in one of three ways: either He will give what is asked for, or He will save it for the Hereafter, or He will ward off an equivalent evil from him.

If one has made supplication and not received evidence of an answer, then one must return with stronger faith and trust and call again and again. When one calls upon Allah for worldly provision and property one must equally strive in the world looking for appropriate opportunity and openings (53:40), (99:7).

That (the fruit of) his striving will soon come in sight.

And anyone who has done an atom's weight of good, shall see it!

The believer trusts that Allah knows and desires the best for us at all times. Thus he delegates his needs and future to Allah's Will whilst striving for the best. In this quest the believer emulates the Prophetic model in action, thought and state. Muhammad (*pbuh*) exemplified the perfect universal being. He was the Qur'an, the discerner between falsehood and truth and the religion itself, walking on earth. There is nothing better for us in this world than to attain knowledge and awareness of Allah's ever-presence, mercy and love and that He knows what is best for us and will give us that which is appropriate and deserved, for He is the All-Just.

Supplication of Allah's Names and Attributes

Allah's mercy is wider and greater than we think. Yet in our earthly state, our needs can be diverse and specific. Thus, we are in constant need to alleviate pain or harm, or to bring about the desired goodness. Calling upon His Names and Attributes is a means of acknowledging our weakness of and turning to the desirable quality of the Name or Attribute so as to submerge ourselves fully in the quality called upon.

As the most desirable qualities in this life are those ascribed to the Creator, we human beings wish to acquire aspects of these qualities to varying degrees, according to the circumstances we are in. There are, however, general tendencies in the human state that cause some of us to become more connected with a particular attribute. Connection with a particular attribute usually comes about because of the special quality of that attribute, or to complement states or conditions in the person's character.

Throughout the Muslim world it has become a custom when a child is born to ask a learned man or sage to name the child. With insight and inspiration the name will reflect the natural tendency, future orientation, or need of the child. It is hoped that by attaching a Divine Attribute to the name of the child it will become his or her dominant trait. As an example: 'Abd al-Rahmān (Servant of the All-Merciful) is given to a child to enhance tendencies of clemency and tenderness, or to a child who possesses a very benign and generous disposition. 'Abd al-Hakim (servant of the most Wise), may be given to a child who clearly shows the potential for wisdom and knowledge, or in the hope that this quality will be reflected in his life. Most Muslim communities live, invoke and interact with constant reference to Allah and His Attributes to which they aspire. In this way, it can be seen that Muslim societies are constantly performing collective supplication.

In conclusion all human needs and shortcomings which lead to supplication are none other than part of Allah's subtle mercy to bring His creation's attention and awareness back to

Him. Allah declared that He was a hidden treasure and He loved to be known and thus He created. Our needs are part of His design to be known and the ultimate purpose of supplication and calling is to express our weakness and dependence on Him. Our actions are only part of the worship of Him; while His gifts and mercy are aspects of His love, grace and generosity, and their occasional coincidence is part of His wisdom.

The awakened person of excellence sees in supplication the opportunity to call upon the true Beloved and is not veiled from the Source, when rejoicing as the fruits of his calling manifest themselves. He who knows the self knows His Lord and loves Him with unconditional passion and dedication.

المقدمة

بِسْمِ اللَّـهِ الرَّحْمَـٰنِ الرَّحِيمِ

الْحَمْدُ للَّـهِ رَبِّ الْعَالَمِيْنَ وَالصَّلاةُ وَالسَّلامُ عَلَى سَيِّدِ الْمُرْسَلِيْنَ وَعَلَى آلِهِ وَأَصْحَابِهِ الْمُنْتَجَبِيْنَ، قَالَ الله تَعَالَى أَلا بِذِكْرِ اللَّهِ تَطْمَئِنُّ الْقُلُوبُ، أَدْعُو اللَّهَ أَنْ تَكُونَ مِنْ زُمْرَةِ الْمُطْمَئِنِّيْنَ الْوَارِدِينَ الْعَارِفِيْنَ الْوَاصِلِيْنَ لِلرَّحْمَةِ الَّتِي لَيْسَ لَهَا انْقِطَاعٌ، لَقَدْ مَنَّ اللَّه عَلَيْنَا بِالْجُودِ وَالْكَرَمِ لِتَمْكِينِنا بِالتَّنَوِّرِ بِما قَدَّمَهُ لَنا خَاتِمُ الأَنْبِيَاءِ وَوَصِيُّهُ أَمِيرُ الْمُؤْمِنِيْنَ عَلِيُّ بْنُ أَبِي طَالِبٍ وَالَّذِينَ اتَّبَعُوهُ فِي الإِحْسَانِ أَقْدِمُ هَذَا الْوِرْدَ الشَّرِيفِ لِمَنْ يَوَدُّ أَنْ يَرِدَ مِنْ ذَخِيرَةِ الْمَعَادِ وَلَا حَوْلَ وَلَا قُوَّةَ إِلَّا بِاللَّهِ الْعَظِيمِ وَلَا غَالِبَ إِلَّا هُوَ وَلَا مَوْجُودَ إِلَّا هُوَ وَلَا مَطْلُوبَ إِلَّا هُوَ وَلَا مَحْبُوبَ إِلَّا هُوَ

يَا هُوَ يَا هُوَ يَا مَنْ

لا هُوَ إِلا هُوَ

الشيخ فضل اللَّهِ الحائرى

Introduction to Litany

In the Name of Allah, the Beneficent, the Merciful. Praise belongs to Allah, the Lord of the worlds. May peace and prayers be showered upon the Master of the Messengers and his household and guided companions. Allah, the Sublime says: "Indeed through the remembrance of Allah the hearts become tranquil." (13:28.) I ask Allah that you be of those whose hearts are tranquil and of those who have arrived and attained the knowledge of Allah and connected themselves to His mercy which is without end.

Allah has bestowed His generosity and munificence upon us by granting us access to enlightenment through the teachings and guidance of the Seal of the Prophets and his vicegerent 'Ali ibn Abi talib and those who followed him in righteousness.

I present this Litany (*wird*) to whomsoever desires access to the treasures of the Hereafter. There is no power and no strength except through Allah, the Magnificent. There is no victor except Him. There is no presence except His. There is nothing and none sought after besides Him. There is no beloved except Him. Oh He, Oh He, Oh He who there is no he except He.

Shaykh Fadhlalla Haeri

Litany

أَعُوذُ بِاللهِ السَّمِيعِ العَلِيمِ مِنَ الشَّيْطَانِ الرَّجِيمِ
(3 مَرَّات)

A'oodhu billaahis-samee 'il-'aleemi minash-shaytaanir-ra-jeem (x 3)

I seek refuge with Allah, the All-hearing, the All-see-ing, from the accursed shaytan. (x 3)

بِسْمِ اللّٰـهِ الرَّحْمَـٰنِ الرَّحِيمِ (3 مَرَّات)

Bismillaahir-rahmaanir-raheem   (x 3)

In the Name of Allah, the most Beneficent, the most Merciful.

اللّٰهم إِنِّي أَسْأَلُكَ بِرَحْمَتِكَ الَّتِي وَسِعَتْ كِلِ شيءٍ

Allahumma innee as'aluka bi-rahmatik al latee wasi`at kulla shay'

Oh Allah, I ask You by Your mercy, which embraces all things;

وَبِقُدْرَتِكَ التي قَهَرْتَ بِها كِل شيءٍ ﴿وَخَضَعَ لها كُلُّ شيءٍ

Wa bi-qudratik al latee qaharta bihaa kulla shay' Wa khada 'a lahaa kullu shay'

and by Your strength, through which You dominate all things, and toward which all things are humble

وَذَلَّ لها كُلُّ شيءٍ وَبِجَبَرُوتِكَ الَّتِي غَلَبْتَ بِها كِل شيءٍ

Wa dhal la lahaa kullu shay' Wa bi-jabarootik al latee ghal-abta bihaa kulla shay'

and before which all things are lowly; by Your invinci-bility, through which You overwhelm all things,

وَبِعِزَّتِكَ الَّتِى لَا يَقُومُ لَهَا شيءٌ وَبِعَظَمَتِكَ الَّتِى مَلَأَتْ
كُلَّ شَىءٍ وَبِنُورِ وَجْهِكَ الَّذِى أَضَاءَ لَهُ كُلُّ شَىءٍ

Wa bi-'izzatik al latee laa ya qoomu lahaa shay' Wa bi-'ad-hamatik al latee mala'at kulla shay' Wa bi-noori waj-hik al ladhee adaa'a lahu kullu shay'

by Your might, which nothing can resist; by Thy tremendousness which has filled all things and by the light of Your face, through which all things are illuminated!

يَا نُورُ يَا قُدُّوسُ يَا أَوَّلَ الْأَوَّلِينَ وَآخِرَ الْأَخِرِينَ

Yaa Nooru, Yaa Qud-doos Yaa Aw-walal, Aw-waleen Wa Aakhiral-aakhireen

Oh Light! Oh Sacred! Oh First of those who are first and Last of those who are last!

يَارَبُّ يَارَبُّ يَارَبُّ يَا كَرِيمُ يَا كَرِيمُ يَا كَرِيمُ

Yaa Rabbu! Yaa Rabbu! Yaa Rabb! Yaa Kareemu! Yaa Kareemu! Yaa Kareem!

Oh Lord! Oh Lord! Oh Lord!
Oh All-generous! Oh All-generous! Oh All-generous!

بِرَحْمَتِكَ يَا أَرْحَمَ الرَّاحِمِينَ

Bi-Rahmatika Yaa arhamar-raahimeen

By Your mercy, Oh Most Merciful of the merciful.

أَسْأَلُكَ بِحَقِّكَ وَقُدْسِكَ وَأَعْظَمِ صِفَاتِكَ وَأَسْمَائِكَ

As'aluka bi-haqqika wa qudsika wa a'adhami sifaatika wa asmaa'ik

I ask You by Your Truth, Your Holiness and the greatest of Your Attributes and Names;

اَنْ تَجْعَلَ أَوْقاتي فِي اللَّيْلِ وَالنَّهَارِ بِذِكْرِكَ مَعْمُورَةٌ

An taja'ala awqaatee fil-layli wan-nahaari bi-dhikrika ma'amoorah

that You make my nights and days filled with Your remembrance

وَبِخِدْمَتِكَ مَوْصُولَةً وَأَعْمَالَى عِنْدَكَ مَــقْبولَةً

Wa bi-khid matika mawsoolah wa a'amaalee 'indaka maqboolah

and joined to Your service and my actions accept-able to You,

حَتَّى تَكُونَ أَعْمَالِي وَأَوْرادى كُلُّها وِرْداً واحِداً

Hat-taa takoona àamaalee wa awraadee kulluhaa wirdan waahida

so that my actions and my litanies may all be a single litany.

يَارَبُّ يَارَبُّ يَارَبُّ يَا كَرِيمُ يَا كَرِيمُ يَا كَرِيمُ

Yaa Rabbu! Yaa Rabbu! Yaa Rabb! Yaa Kareemu! Yaa Ka-reemu! Yaa Kareem!

Oh Lord! Oh Lord! Oh Lord!
Oh All-generous! Oh All-generous! Oh All-generous!

بِرَحْمَتِكَ يَا أَرْحَمَ الرَّاحِمِيْنَ إِنَّكَ قَادِرٌ عَلَى مَا تَشَاءُ

Bi-Rahmatika Yaa arhamar-raahimeen Innaka qaadirun 'alaa maa tashaa'

By Your mercy, Oh Most Merciful of the merciful!
Surely You have power over all things.

تُؤْتِى الْمُلْكَ لِمَنْ تَشَاءُ وَتَنْزِعُ الْمُلْكَ مِمَّن تَشَاءُ

Tu'teel-mulka liman tashaa' Wa tanzi'ul-mulka mim man tashaa'

You give the kingdom to whom You will,
and You seize the kingdom from whom You will;

وَتُعِزُّ مَن تَشَاءُ وَتُذِلُّ مَن تَشَاءُ

Wa tu 'izzu man tashaa' Wa tudhil lu man tashaa'

You exalt whom You will, and You abase whom You will;

بِيَدِكَ الْخَيْرُ إِنَّكَ عَلَى كُلِّ شَىْءٍ قَدِيرٌ

Bi-yadikal-khayru in-naka 'alaa kulli shay'in Qadeer

in Your hand is the good; You are powerful over all things.

تُولِجُ اللَّيْلَ فِى النَّهَارِ وَتُولِجُ النَّهَارَ فِى اللَّيْلِ

Toolijul-layla fin-nahaari wa toolijun-nahaara fil-layl

You make the night enter into the day and the day enter into the night;

وَتُخْرِجُ الْحَىَّ مِنَ الْمَيِّتِ وَتُخْرِجُ الْمَيِّتَ مِنَ الْحَىِّ

Wa tukhrijul-hayya min al-mayyiti wa tukhrijul-mayyita min Al-hayy

You bring forth the living from the dead and You bring forth the dead from the living;

وَتَرْزُقُ مَنْ تَشَاءُ بِغَيْرِ حِسَابٍ

Wa tarzuqu man tashaa'u bi-ghayri hisaab

and You provide for whomsoever You will without reckoning.

لَا إِلَهَ إِلَّا أَنْتَ سُبْحَانَكَ اللَّهُمَّ وبِحَمْدِكَ

Laa ilaaha illaa anta subhaanaka allaahumma wa bi-hamdik
There is no god but You! Glory be to You & Yours is the praise!

يَارَبُّ يَارَبُّ يَارَبُّ يَا كَرِيمُ يَا كَرِيمُ يَا كَرِيمُ

Yaa Rabbu! Yaa Rabbu! Yaa Rabb!
Yaa Kareemu! Yaa Kareemu! Yaa Kareem!
Oh Lord! Oh Lord! Oh Lord!
Oh All-generous, Oh All-generous, Oh All-generous!

بِرَحْمَتِكَ يَا أَرْحَمَ الرَّاحِمِيْنَ

Bi-Rahmatika Yaa arhamar-raahimeen
By Your mercy, Oh Most Merciful of the merciful!

اللَّهُمَّ إِنِّي أَسْأَلُكَ بِاسْمِكَ اللَّهِ الرَّحْمَٰنِ الرَّحِيم

Allaahumma innee as'aluka bismik-allaahir-rahmaanir-raheem
Oh Allah, I ask You by Your Name, Allah, the All-Benef-icent, All-Merciful!

يَا ذَا الْجَلَالِ والإِكْرَامِ يَا حَيُّ يَا قَيُّومُ يَا لَا إِلَهَ إِلا أَنْتَ

Yaa dhal-jalaali wal-ikraam, Yaa hayyu, yaa qayyoom
Yaa laa ilaaha illa ant
Oh Possessor of majesty and splendour! Oh Living! Oh Self- subsistent! Oh You whom there is no god but You!

يَا هُوَ يَا مَنْ لَا يَعْلَمُ مَا هُوَ وَلَا كَيْفَ هُوَ

Yaa huwa, yaa man laa ya'alamu maa huwa Wa laa kayfa huwa,
Oh He! Oh He Whom none knows what He is, nor How He is,

31

وَلَا أَيْنَ هُوَ وَلَا حَيْثُ هُوَ إِلَّا هُوَ

wa laa ayna huwa, Wa laa haythu huwa illaa huwa
nor Where He is, nor in what respect He is but He!

يا ذَا المُلْكِ وَالْمَلَكُوتِ يا ذَا الْعِزَّةِ وَالْجَبَرُوتِ

Yaa dhal-mulki wal-malakoot, yaa dhal-'izzati wal-jabaroot
Oh Possessor of the dominion and the kingdom! Oh
Possessor of might and invincibility!

يا مَلِكُ ياقُدُّوسُ يا سَلَامُ يا مُؤْمِنُ يا مُهَيْمِنُ يا عَزِيزُ

*Yaa maliku, yaa qud-doosu, yaa salaamu, yaa mu'minu, yaa
muhaymin Yaa 'azeezu,*
Oh King! Oh All-sacred! Oh Peace! Oh All-faithful!
Oh All-preserver! Oh All-mighty!

يا جَبَّارُ يَا مُتَكَبِّرُ يا خَالِقُ يا بارِئُ يا مصوّرُ يا مُفِيدُ

*yaa jab-baaru, yaa mutakab-biru, yaa khaaliqu, yaa
baari' Yaa musaw-wiru, yaa mufeedu,*
Oh All-compeller! Oh All-sublime! Oh Creator! Oh
Maker! Oh Shaper! Oh Benefiter!

يا مُدَبِّرُ يا شَدِيدُ يا مُبْدِئُ يا مُعِيدُ يا مُبِيدُ يا وَدُودُ

yaa mudab-biru, yaa shadeedu, yaa mubdi'
Yaa mu`eedu, yaa mubeedu, yaa wadoodu,
Oh Director! Oh Severe! Oh Originator!
Oh Returner! Oh Destroyer! Oh All-loving!

يا مَحْمُودُ يا مَعْبُودُ يا بَعِيدُ يا قَرِيبُ يا مُجِيبُ يا رَقِيبُ

*yaa mahmoodu, yaa ma`abood Yaa ba`eedu, yaa qareebu, yaa
mujeebu, yaa raqeebu,*
Oh All-praiseworthy! Oh All-worshipful!
Oh Far! Oh Near! Oh Responder! Oh Watcher!

ياحسيبُ يا بَدِيعُ يا رفِيعُ يا منِيعُ يا سميعُ يا عَلِيمُ

yaa haseeb Yaa badee'u, yaa rafee'u, yaa manee'u, yaa samee'u, yaa 'aleem

Oh Reckoner! Oh Innovator! Oh Exalter! Oh Preventer! Oh All-hearing! Oh All-knowing!

يا حَلِيمُ يا كَرِيمُ يا حَكِيمُ يا قدِيمُ يَا عَلِيُّ يا عَظِيمُ

Yaa haleemu, yaa kareemu, yaa hakeemu, yaa qadeemu, yaa 'alee Yaa 'adheemu,

Oh All-clement! Oh All-generous! Oh All-wise! Oh Eternal! Oh Most High! Oh Magnificent!

يا حَنَّانُ يا مَنَّانُ يَا دَيانُ يا مُسْتَعَانُ يا جَلِيلُ يا جَمِيلُ

yaa han-naanu, yaa man-naanu, yaa day-yaanu, yaa musta'aan Yaa jaleelu, yaa jameelu,

Oh All-comforting! Oh All-gracious! Oh Accounter! Oh Recourse! Oh All-majestic! Oh All-beautiful!

يا وَكِيلُ يا كَفِيلُ يَا مُقِيلُ يا مُنِيلُ يَا نَبِيلُ يَا دَلِيلُ

yaa wakeelu, yaa kafeelu, yaa muqeel Yaa muneelu, yaa nabeelu, yaa daleelu,

Oh Guardian! Oh Surety! Oh Annuller! Oh Obtainer! Oh All-noble! Oh Leader!

يا هَادِى يا بَادِى يا اَوَّلُ يا آخِرُ يا ظاهِرُ يا باطِنُ يا قائِمُ

yaa haadi'u, yaa baadi' Yaa aw-walu, yaa aakhiru, yaa dhaa-hiru, yaa baatinu, yaa qaa'im

Oh Guide! Oh All-apparent! Oh First! Oh Last! Oh Outward! Oh Inward! Oh All-steadfast!

يا دَائِمُ يا عَالِمُ يا حَاكِمُ يا قاضِي يا عادِلُ يا فاصِلُ

Yaa da'imu, yaa 'aalimu, yaa haakimu, yaa qaadee, yaa 'aadil
Yaa faasilu,
Oh Everlasting! Oh Knower! Oh Decider! Oh Judge!
Oh Just! Oh Separator!

يا واصِلُ يا طاهِرُ يَا مُطَهِّرُ يا قادِرُ يا مُقْتَدِرُ يا كَبِيرُ

yaa waasilu, yaa taahiru, yaa mutah-hiru, yaa qaadir
Yaa muq-tadiru, yaa kabeeru,
Oh Joiner! Oh Pure! Oh Purifier! Oh All-powerful!
Oh All-able! Oh All-great!

يا مُتَكَبِّرُ يا واحِدُ يَا أَحَدُ يا صَمَدُ يا مَنْ لَمْ يَلِدْ وَلَمْ
يُولَدْ

yaa muta-kabbiru, yaa waahidu, yaa ahad
Yaa samadu, Yaa man lam yalid wa lam yoolad,
Oh All-sublime! Oh One! Oh Unique! Oh Everlasting
Refuge! Oh He Who begets not and was not begotten,

وَلَمْ يَكُنْ لَهُ كُفُواً أَحَدُ يا مَنْ عَلِيَ فَقَهَرَ

wa lam yakul lahu kufuwan ahad Yaa man 'ale-ya fa-qahar
and equal to whom there is none.
Oh He who is exalted and dominates!

يا مَنْ مَلَكَ فَقَدَرَ يا مَنْ بَطَنَ فَخَبَرَ

Yaa man malaka fa-qadar Yaa man batana fa-khabar
Oh He who is master and exercises power!
Oh He who is inward and aware!

يَا مَنْ عُبِدَ فَشَكَرَ يَا مَنْ عُصِيَ فَغَفَرَ

Yaa man 'ubida fa-shakar Yaa man 'usiya fa-ghafar
Oh He who is worshipped and thankful!
Oh He who is disobeyed and forgives!

يَا مَنْ لَا تَحْوِيهِ الفِكَرُ وَلَا يُدْرِكُهُ بَصَرُ

Yaa man laa tahweehil-fikaru, wa laa yudrikuhu basarun,
Oh He who is not encompassed by thoughts, nor perceived by vision;

وَلَا يَخْفَى عَلَيْهِ آثَرُ

Wa laa yakhfaa 'alayhi aathar
and from whom no trace remains hidden!

يَا رَازِقَ الْبَشَرِ يَا مُقَدِّرَ كُلِّ قَدَرٍ يَا عَالِيَ الْمَكَانِ

*Yaa raaziqal-bashar Yaa muqad-dira kulli qa-dar
Yaa 'aaleeyal-makaan*
Oh Provider of mankind! Oh Determiner of every lot!
Oh Lofty of place!

يَا شَدِيدَ الأَرْكَانِ يَا مُبَدِّلَ الزَّمَانِ يَا قَابِلَ الْقُرْبَانِ

*Yaa shadeedal-arkaan Yaa mubaddilaz-zamaan Yaa qaabil
al-qurbaan*
Oh Firm in supports! Oh Transformer of Time!
Oh Acceptor of sacrifices!

يَا ذَا الْمَنِّ وَالْإِحْسَانِ يَا ذَا الْعِزَّةِ وَالسُّلْطَانِ

Yaa dhal-manni wal-ihsaan Yaa dhal-'izzati was-sultaan
Oh Possessor of graciousness and benevolence!
Oh Possessor of might and force!

35

يا رَحيمُ يا رحمنُ يا مَنْ هُوَ كُل يَومٍ فى شَأْنٍ

Yaa raheemu, yaa rahmaan Yaa man huwa kulla yawmin fee sha'n

Oh All-compassionate! Oh All-merciful!
Oh He who is every day upon some labour!

يا مَنْ لا يَشْغِلُهُ شَأنٌ عن شَأنٍ

Yaa man laa yashghu lihu sha'nun `an sha'n

Oh He who is not distracted from one labour by another!

يا عَظيمَ الشَّأنِ يا مَنْ هُوَ بِكُلِّ مَكَانٍ

Yaa 'adheem ash-sha'n Yaa man huwa bi-kulli makaan

Oh Tremendous in rank! Oh He who is in every place

يا سَامِعَ الأَصْواتِ يا مُجِيبَ الدَّعَواتِ يا مُنْجِحَ الطَّلِباتِ

Yaa saami'a al-awaat Yaa mujeeb ad-da'awaat Yaa munjih at-talibaat

Oh He who hears all sounds! Oh He who answers all supplications!

يا قاضِيَ الحاجاتِ يا مُنْزِلَ الْبَرَكاتِ يا راحِمَ الْعَبَراتِ

Yaa qaadeey al-haajaat Yaa munzil al-barakaat raa-hima al-`abaraat

Oh He who provides all needs! Oh He who sends down blessings! Oh He who has mercy upon tears!

يا مُقيلَ الْعَثَراتِ يا كَاشِفَ الْكُرُباتِ يا وَلِيَ الْحَسَناتِ

Yaa muqeel al-'atharaat Yaa kaashif al-kurubaat Yaa waleey al-hasanaat

Oh He who cancels out false steps! Oh He who removes troubles! Oh He who sponsors good things!

يا رافِعَ الدَّرَجاتِ يا مُؤْتِيَ السُّؤُلاتِ يا مُحْيِي الأَمْواتِ

Yaa raafi'ad-darajaat Yaa mu'teey as-su'laat Yaa muh-yee al-amwaat

Oh He who exalts in rank! Oh He who bestows requests! Oh He who gives life to the dead!

يا جامِعَ الشَّتاتِ يا مُطَّلِعَ النِّيَّاتِ يا رَادٍ ما قَدْ فاتَ

Yaa jaami'ash-shataat Yaa mut-tali'an 'al-an-neeyaat Yaa raad-damaa qad faat

Oh He who gathers all scattered things! Oh He who is aware of all intentions! Oh He who brings back what has passed away!

يا أَجْوَدَ الأَجْوَدِينَ يا أَكْرَمَ الأَكْرَمِينَ

Yaa aj wadal-aj wadeen Yaa akramal-akrameen

Oh Most Munificent of the most munificent! Oh Most Generous of the most generous!

يا غِياثَ الْمُسْتَغِيثِينَ يا غايَةَ الطالبينَ

Yaa ghiyaathal-mustaghee-theen Yaa ghaa-yatat-taalibeen

Oh Helper of those who seek aid! Oh Goal of the seekers!

يَارَبُّ يَارَبُّ يَارَبُّ يَا كَرِيمُ يَا كَرِيمُ يَا كَرِيمُ

Yaa Rabbu! Yaa Rabbu! Yaa Rabb!
Yaa Kareemu! Yaa Kareemu! Yaa Kareem!

Oh Lord! Oh Lord! Oh Lord!
Oh All-generous! Oh All-generous! Oh All-generous!

37

بِرَحْمَتِكَ يَا أَرْحَمَ الرَّاحِمِيْنَ

Bi-Rahmatika Yaa arhamar-raahimeen
By Your mercy, Oh Most Merciful of the merciful!

يا مَنْ يُبْدِى الخَلْقَ ثُمَّ يُعِيدُهُ يا مَنْ إِلَيْهِ يُرْجَعُ
الأَمْرُ كُلُّهُ

Yaa man yubdi'ul-khalqa thumma yu`eeduh
Yaa man ilayhee yurja`ul-amru kulluh
Oh He who brings forth creation then returns it!
Oh He to whom all affairs return!

يا مَنْ أَظْهَرَ فى كُلِّ شَىْءٍ لُطْفَهُ

Yaa man adh-hara fee kulli shay'in lutfah
Oh He who revealed in everything His subtle grace!

يا مَنْ أَحْسَنَ كُلَّ شَىْءٍ خَلْقَهُ

Yaa man ahsana kulla shay'in khalqah
Oh He who perfected everything He created!

يا حَبِيبَ مَنْ لا حَبِيبَ لَهُ يا طَبِيبَ مَنْ لا طَبِيبَ لَهُ

Yaa habeeba man laa habeeba lah, Yaa tabeeba man laa ta-beeba lah
Oh Beloved of him who has no beloved!
Oh Doctor for him who has no doctor!

يا مُجِيب مَنْ لا مُجِيبَ لَهُ يا شَفِيقَ مَن لا شَفِيقَ لَهُ

Yaa mujeeba man laa mujeeba lah, Yaa shafeeqa man laa shafeeqa lah
Oh Answerer to him who has none to answer for him!
Oh Patron for him who has no patron!

يا رَفِيقَ مَنْ لا رَفِيقَ لَهُ يَا مُغِيثَ مَن لا مُغِيثَ لَهُ

*Yaa rafeeqa man laa rafeeqa lah, Yaa mugheetha man laa
mugheetha lah*

Oh Friend for him who has no friend!
Oh Succourer for him who has no succourer!

يا دَليلَ مَنْ لا دَليلَ لـهُ يا أَنِيسَ مَنْ لا أَنِيسَ لَهُ

*Yaa daleela man laa daleela lah, Yaa aneesa man laa
aneesa lah*

Oh Guide for him who has no guide!
Oh Intimate friend for him with no intimate friends!

يا راحِمَ مَنْ لا راحِمَ لَـهُ يا صاحِبَ مَنْ لا صَاحِبَ لَهُ

*Yaa raahima man laa raahima lah, Yaa saahiba man laa
saahiba lah*

Oh Merciful to him for whom there is no merciful!
Oh Companion for him who has no companion!

يا أَوَّلَ كُلِّ شَيْءٍ وَآخِرَهُ يَا إِلَهَ كُلِّ شَيْءٍ وَوَكِيلَهُ

*Yaa awwala kulli shay'in wa aakhirah Yaa ilaaha kulli
shay'in wa wakeelah*

Oh First of everything and the Last!
Oh God of everything and its Trustee!

يا رَبِّ كُلِّ شَيْءٍ وَصانِعَهُ يا بَارِى كُلِّ شَيْءٍ وَفالِقَهُ

*Yaa rabbi kulli shay'in wa saani`ah Yaa bari'a kulli shay'in
wa faaliqah*

Oh Lord of everything and its Producer!
Oh Maker of everything and its Creator

39

يَا قَابِضَ كُلِّ شَيْءٍ وَبَاسِطَهُ يَا مُبْدِئَ كُلِّ شَيْءٍ وَمُعِيدَهُ

Yaa qaabida kulli shay'in wa baasitah Yaa mubdi'a kulli shay'in wa mu`eedah

**Oh Constrictor of everything and its Expander!
Oh Originator of everything and its Returner!**

يَا مُنْشِئَ كُلِّ شَيْءٍ وَمُقَدَّرَهُ يَا مُكَوِّنَ كُلِّ شَيْءٍ وَمُحَوِّلَهُ

Yaa munshi'a kulli shay'in wa mu-qad-darah Yaa mukaw-wina kulli shay'in wa muhaw-wilah

**Oh Establisher of everything and its Apportioner!
Oh Shaper of everything and its Transformer!**

يَا مُحْيِيَ كُلِّ شَيْءٍ وَمُمِيتَهُ يَا خَالِقَ كُلِّ شَيْءٍ وَوَارِثَهُ

Yaa muhyeea kulli shay'in wa moomeetah Yaa khaaliqa kulli shay'in wa waarithah

Oh Bringer to life of everything and its Bringer to death! Oh Creator of everything and its Inheritor!

يَا رَبُّ يَا رَبُّ يَا رَبُّ يَا كَرِيمُ يَا كَرِيمُ يَا كَرِيمُ

*Yaa Rabbu! Yaa Rabbu! Yaa Rabb!
Yaa Kareemu! Yaa Kareemu! Yaa Kareem!*

**Oh Lord! Oh Lord! Oh Lord!
Oh All-generous! Oh All-generous! Oh All-generous!**

بِرَحْمَتِكَ يَا أَرْحَمَ الرَّاحِمِينَ

Bi-Rahmatika Yaa arhamar-raahimeen

By Your mercy, Oh Most Merciful of the merciful!

اللَّهُمَّ إِنِّي أَسْأَلُكَ إِسْلَاماً صَحِيحاً يَصْحَبُهُ الاسْتِسْلَامُ لِأَوَامِرِكَ وَ نَوَاهِيكَ

Allaahumma innee as'aluka Islaaman saheehan yasha-bu-hul-istislaamu li-awaamirika wa nawaaheek,

Oh Allah! We ask You for Sound Islam (submission) accompanied by submission to Your orders and prohibitions;

وَإِيماناً خَالِصاً رَاسِخاً ثَابتاً مَحْفُوظًا مِنْ جَمِيعِ الشُّبَهِ وَالْمَهَالِكِ

Wa eemaanan khaalisan raasikhan thaabitan, mahfoodhan min jamee'ish-shubahi wal-ma haalik,

and for pure Iman (faith with knowledge), firmly established, enduring, protected from all ambiguities and dangers;

وَإِحْسَاناً يَزِجُّ بِنَا فِي حَضَرَاتِ الْغُيُوبِ وَنَتَطَهَّرُ بِهِ مِنْ أَنْوَاعِ الْغَفَلَاتِ وَسَائِرِ الْعُيُوبِ

Wa ihsaanan yazij-ju bina fee hadaraatil-ghuyoobi wa natatahharu bihee min anwaa'il-ghafalaati wa saa'iril-'uyoob,

and for Ihsan that will drive us into the presence of the unseen, may we be purified by it from every kind of negligence & defect;

وَإِيقَاناً يَكْشِفُ لَنَا عَنْ حَضَرَاتِ الأسْمَاءِ وَالصَّفَاتِ

Wa eeqaanan yakshifulana 'an hadaraatil-asmaa'i was-sfaat,

and for the Yaqin (certainty) which will reveal to us the presences of the Names and Attributes

وَيَرْحَلُ بِنَا إِلَى مُشَاهَدَةِ أَنْوَارِ تَجَلِّيَاتِ الذَّاتِ

wa yarr-halu bina ilaa mushaahad-dati anwaari
tajal-leeyaati-dhaat

by which we will be carried into the direct witnessing
of the lights of the self-manifestations of the Essence;

وَعِلْماً نَافِعًا نَفْقَهُ بِهِ كَيْفَ نَتَأَدَّبُ مَعَكَ وَنُنَاجِيكَ فِي
الصَّلَوَاتِ

Wa `ilman naafi`an naf-qahu bihee kayfa nata'addabu
ma `aka wa nunaa-jeeka fis-salawaat,

And for useful `ilm (knowledge) through which we may
understand how to conduct ourselves in Your presence
and how to confide in You in prayer.

وَامْلأُ قُلُوبَنَا بِأَنْوَارِ مَعْرِفَتِكَ حَتَّى نَشْهَدَ قَيُّومِيَّتَكَ
السَّارِيَةَ فِي جَمِيعِ الْمَخْلُوقَاتِ

Wamla' quloobanaa bi-anwaari ma`rifatika hattaa nash-ha-
da qay-yoomee yatakas-saaree-yata fee jamee`il-makhlooqaat,

Fill our hearts with the lights of Your gnosis so that
we may witness Your All-sustaining Gatheredness
flowing in all created things.

واجْعَلْنَا مِنْ أَهْلِ دَائِرَةِ الْفَضْلِ الْمَحْبُونِينَ لَدَيْكَ

Waja `alnaa min ahli daa'iratil-fadlil-mahboobeena ladayk

Let us be among the circle of Your bounty, beloved in
Your presence

وَمِنَ الرَّاسِخِيْنَ الْمُتَمَكِّنِيْنَ فِى التَّوَكُّلِ وَصِدْقِ الْإِعْتِمَادِ عَلَيْكَ

*wa minar-raasikheenal-mutamak-kineena fit-tawakkuli
wa sidqil-i`timaadi `alayk,*

**and among the firmly grounded enduring in trust and
sincerity of dependence on You.**

وَحَقِّقْ رَجَاءَنَا بِالْإِجَابَةِ يَا كَرِيْمُ يَاوَهَّابُ فِى كُلِّ مَا سَأَلْنَاكَ

*Wa haq-qiq rajaa'anaa bil-ijaabati, Yaa kareemu, yaa wah-
haabu fee kulli maa sa'alnaak,*

**Realize our hope with the answer to all that we ask,
Oh All-generous, Oh All-giving! In all that we ask
of you.**

وَلَا تَكِلْنَا يَا مَوْلَانَا فِى جَمِيْعِ حَرَكَاتِنَا وَسَكَنَاتِنَا إِلَى أَحَدٍ سِوَاكَ

*Wa laa takilnaa, yaa mawlaanaa fee jamee`i harakaatinaa
wa saka-naa-tina ilaa ahadin siwaak,*

**Do not, Oh Master, let us rely on any other than You
in stillness or in action.**

فَإِنَّكَ عَوَّدْتَنَا إِحْسَانَكَ مِنَ قَبْلِ سُؤَالِنَا وَنَحْنُ فِى بُطُونِ الْأُمَّهَاتِ

*Fa'innaka `awwad-tanaa ihsaanaka min qabli su'aalinaa wa
nahnu fee butoonil-ummahaat,*

**You have accustomed us to Your perfect generosity
before we even asked for it while we were in our
mother's wombs.**

وَرَبَّيْتَنَا بِلَطِيفِ رُبُوبِيَّتِكَ تَرْبِيَةً تَقْصُرُ عَنْ إِدْرَاكِهَا
الْعُقُوْلُ الْمُنَوَّرَاتُ

*Wa rab-baytanaa bi-lateefi ruboobeeyyatika tarbeeyatan
taqsuru `an idraakihal-`uqoolul-munaw-waraat,*

You have raised us with the subtle grace of Your lord-
ship over existence in a manner far beyond the percep-
tion of illuminated intellects.

فَنَسْأَلُكَ اللّٰهُمَّ بِنَبِيِّكَ الَّذِى فَضَّلْتَهُ عَلَى سَائِرِ الْأَنْبِيَاءِ
وَالْمُرْسَلِينَ

*Fanas'aluka allaahumma bi-nabeeyikal-ladhee fad-dal tahu
`alaa saa'iril-ambiyaa'i wal-mursaleen,*

We ask You, Oh Allah, by Your Prophet, whom You
have preferred above all other prophets and
messengers,

وَبِرَسُولِكَ الَّذِى جَعَلْتَ رِسَالَتَهُ عَامَّةً وَرَحْمَةً لِلْخَلَائِقِ
أَجْمَعِينَ

*Wa bi-rasoolikal-ladhee ja`alta risaala-tahu `aam-matan
wa rahmatan lil-khalaa'iqi ajma`een,*

And by Your Messenger whose message You made
universal and a mercy to all creation

أَنْ تُصَلِّىَ وَتُسَلِّمَ عَلَيْهِ وَعَلَى آلِهِ صَلَاةً وَسَلَاماً

*An tusalleeya wa tusal-lima `alayhi wa `ala aalihi salaatun
wa salaaman*

to bless him and his family and grant them a peace

نَنَالُ بِهِمَا مَحَبَّتَهُ وَمُتَابَعَتَهُ فِى الْأَقْوَال والأفعال

nanaalu bihimaa mahabbatahu, Wa mutaaba`atahu
fil-aqwaali wal-af`aali

by which we may attain his love and follow him in
words, deeds,

وَالْمُرَاقَبَةِ وَالْمُشَاهَدَةِ والآدَابِ وَالْأَخْلاقِ وَالْأَحْوَال

wal-muraaqa-bati wal-mushaahad-dati wal-aadaabi
wal-akhlaaqi wal-ahwaal

in watching-practice, witnessing, courtesy, morals and
states.

وَنَسْأَلُكَ يَا مَوْلانَا بِجَاهِهِ أَنْ تَهَبَ لَنَا عِلْماً نَافِعًا يَنْتَفِعُ
بِهِ كُلُّ سَامِعُ

Wa nas'aluka yaa mawlaanaa bi-jaahihee an tahaba lanaa
`ilman naafi`an yan-tafi`u bihee kullu saami`

We ask You, Oh Master, by his rank, to grant us that
useful knowledge through which every listener may
profit

وتَخْشَعُ لَهُ الْقُلُوبُ وَتَقْشَعِرُّ مِنْهُ الجُلُودُ وَتَجْرِى لَهُ
المَدَامِعُ

Wa takhsha`u lahul-quloobu wa taqsha`irru minhul-juloodu
wa tajree lahul-madaami`

and every heart may be made humble, and at which
the skin may thrill and the tears flow.

إِنَّكَ أَنتَ القَادِرُ المُرِيدُ الْعَالِمُ الْحَيُّ الوَاسِعُ

Innaka antal-qaadirul-mureedul-`aalimul-hayyul-waasi`

You are the All-powerful, the Willful, the Knowing,
the Living, the Vast.

سُبْحَانَ رَبِّكَ رَبِّ الْعِزَّةِ عَمَّا يَصِفُونَ وَسَلَامٌ عَلَى
الْمُرْسَلِينَ وَالْحَمْدُ اللهِ رَبِّ الْعَالَمِينَ

*Subhaana rabbika rabbil-`izzati `ammaa yasifoon Wa salaa-
mun `alal-mursaleen wal-hamdu lillaahi rabbil-`aalameen*

Glory be to your Lord, the Lord of might, above all that
they describe, and peace be upon the messengers, and
praise belongs to Allah, the Lord of the worlds.

يَارَبُّ يَارَبُّ يَارَبُّ يَا كَرِيمُ يَا كَرِيمُ يَا كَرِيمُ

Yaa Rabbu! Yaa Rabbu! Yaa Rabb!
Yaa Kareemu! Yaa Kareemu! Yaa Kareem!
Oh Lord! Oh Lord! Oh Lord!
Oh All-generous! Oh All-generous! Oh All-generous!

بِرَحْمَتِكَ يَا أَرْحَمَ الرَّاحِمِينَ

Bi-Rahmatika Yaa arhamar-raahimeen
By Your Mercy, Oh Most Merciful of the Merciful

لا إله الاالله (10 مَرَّات)

Laa ilaaha illa-llaah (x 10)
There is no god but Allah. (x 10)

لا إله الاالله مُحَمَّدٌ رَسُولُ اللَّه (3 مَرَّات)

Laa ilaaha illa-llaah muhammadur rasoolul-llaah (x 3)
There is no god but Allah and Muhammad is His Messenger. (x3)

اللهُ لَطِيفٌ بِعِبَادِهِ يَرْزُقُ مَنْ يَشَاءُ وَهُوَ القَوِيُّ العَزِيزُ
(10 مَرَّات)

Allaahu lateefun bi-`ibaadihee yar-zuqu man yashaa'u wa huwal-qaweeyul-`azeez (x 10)

Allah is Latif with His slaves. He gives wealth to whom He chooses, and He is the Strong, the Inestimably Precious. (x 10)

أَلَا يَا لَطِيفُ يَا لَطِيفُ لَكَ اللُّطْفُ فَأَنْتَ اللَّطِيفُ

Alaa yaa lateefu yaa lateefu lakal-lutfu fa-antal-lateefu

Alaa ya Latifu, ya Latifu, the lutf is Yours!
You are the Latif,

مِنْكَ يَشْمَلُنَا اللُّطْفُ لَطِيفٌ لَطِيفٌ إِنَّنِي مُتَوَسِّلٌ
بِلُطْفِكَ

minka yashmalunal-lutfu lateefu lateefu innanee mutawas-silun bi-lutfika

and from You the lutf engulfs us. Latifu, Latifu, I beg You by Your lutf

فَالْطِفْ بِي وَقَدْ نَزَلَ اللُّطْفُ بِلُطْفِكَ عُدْنَا يَا لَطِيفُ

fal tuf bee wa qad nazalal-lutfu bi-lutfika 'udhnaa yaa lateefu

be the lutf to me - and the lutf has descended!
Ya Latifu, we have hidden in Your lutf -

وَهَا نَحْنُ دَخَلْنَا فِي وَسْطِ اللُّطْفِ وَانْسَدَلَ اللُّطْفُ

wa haa nahnu da khalnaa fi wastil-lutfi wan-sadalal-lutfu

we have gone into the centre of lutf - and the lutf has descended!

نَجونَا بِلُطفِ اللّٰهِ ذِى اللُّطِفِ إِنَّهُ لَطِيفٌ لَطِيفٌ

najawnaa bi-lutfil-llaahi dhil-lutfi innahu lateefun lateefun
**We have been freed by the lutf of Allah, the Possessor
of lutf, Latifu, Latifu,**

لُطْفُهُ دَائِماً لُطفُ

lutfuhu daa'iman lutfu
His lutf is always that.

أَلَا يا حَفِيظُ يا حَفِيظُ لَكَ الْحِفْظُ فَأَنْتَ الْحَفِيظُ

*alaa yaa hafeedhu yaa hafeedhu lakal-hifdhu fa-antal-
hafeedhu*
**Alaa Ya Hafidhu, ya Hafidhu, the hifdh is Yours!
You are the Hafidhu,**

مِنْكَ يَشْمَلُنَا الْحِفْظُ حَفِيظٌ حَفِيظٌ إِنَّنَا نَتَوَسَّلُ
بِحِفْظِكَ

*minka yashmalunaal-hifdhu hafeedhun hafeedhun innanaa
nata-wassalu bi-hifdhika*
**and from You the hifdh engulfs us.
Hafidhu, Hafidhu, I beg You by Your hifdh –**

فَاحْفَظْنَا وَ قَدْ نَزَلَ الْحِفْظُ بِحِفْظِكَ عُدْنَا يا حَفِيظُ

*fah fadhnaa wa qad nazalal-hifdhu bi-hifdhika 'udhnaa yaa
hafeedhu*
**be the hifdh to me – and the hifdh has descended.
Hafidhu, we have hidden in Your hifdh –**

وَهَا نَحْنُ دَخَلْنَا فِي وَسْطِ الْحِفْظِ وَانْسَدَلَ الْحِفْظِ

wa haa nahnu da khalnaa fi-wastil-hifdhi wan sadalal-hifdhu

we have gone into the centre of hifdh - and the hifdh has descended.

نَجَوْنَا بِحِفْظِ اللهِ ذِى الْحِفْظِ إِنَّهُ حَفِيظٌ حَفِيظٌ

najawnaa bi-hif dhil-llaahi dhil-hifdhi innahu hafeedhun hafeedhun

We have been freed by the hifdh of Allah, the Possessor of hifdh. Hafidhu, Hafidhu,

حِفْظُهُ دَائِماً حِفْظُ بِجَاهِ إِمَامِ الْمُرْسَلِينَ مُحَمَّدٍ

hifdhuhu daa'iman hifdhu bi-jaahi imaamil-mursaleena muhammadin

His hifdh is always that. By the rank of the Imam of the messengers, Muhammad,

فَلَوْلَاهُ عَيْنُ الْحِفْظِ مَا نَزَلَ الْحِفْظُ عَلَيْهِ صَلَةُ اللَّهِ

fa-law laahu `aynul-hifdhi maa nazalal-hifdhu `alayhi salaatul-llaahi

were he not the source of the hifdh, then it would not have descended. Blessings be upon him

مَا قَالَ مُنْشِدٌ أَلَا يَا حَفِيظُ يَا حَفِيظٌ لَكَ الْحِفْظُ

maa qaala munshidun alaa yaa hafeedhu yaa hafeedhu lakal-hifdhu

as long as there is one who chants:
'Ya Hafidhu, ya Hafidhu, the hifdh is Yours!'

لا إله الا االلَّه (10 مَرَّات)

Laa ilaaha illa-llaah (x 10)
There is no god but Allah! (x 10)

لا إله الا االلَّه مُحَمَّدُ رَسُولُ اللَّهِ

Laa ilaaha illa-llaah muhammadur rasoolul-llaah
There is no god but Allah, Muhammad is the Messenger of Allah.

أَعُوذُ بِاللَّهِ السَّمِيْعِ العَلِيْمِ مِنَ الشَّيْطَانِ الرَّجِيمِ

A`oodhu billaahis-samee`il-`aleemi minash-shaytaanir-ra-
jeem
I seek refuge in Allah, the All-hearing, the All-knowing, from the accursed Shaytan.

بِسْمِ اللَّهِ الرَّحْمَـٰنِ الرَّحِيمِ

Bismillaahir-rahmaanir-raheem
In the name of Allah, the Beneficent, the Merciful

اَللهُمَّ إِنَّ مَغْفِرَتَكَ أَرْجَى مِنْ عَمَلِي وَإِنَّ رَحْمَتَكَ
أَوْسَعُ مِنْ ذَنْبِي

Allaahumma inna maghfirataka atjaa min`amalee wa inna
rahmataka aw-sa`u min dhanbee
Oh Allah, surely Your forgiveness is more hoped for
than my actions. And surely Your mercy is vaster than
my sins.

اَللهُمَّ إِنْ كَانَ ذَنْبِي عِنْدَكَ عَظِيماً فَمَغْفِرَتُكَ
أَعْظَمُ مِنْ ذَنْبِي

Allaahumma in kaana dhanbee`indaka`adheeman famagh-
firatuka a`adhamu min dhanbee

Oh Allah, if my sin be considered great by You, Your
pardon is greater than my sin.

اللهُمَّ إِنْ لَمْ أَكُنْ أَهْلاً أَنْ أَبْلُغَ رَحْمَتَكَ فَرَحْمَتُكَ
أَهْلٌ أَنْ تَبْلُغَنِي وَتَسَعْنِي لأنها وَسِعَتْ كُلِّ شَيْءٍ

Allaahumma in lam akun ahlan an ablugha rahmataka farah
mataka ahlun an tablughanee wa tasa`anee li-annahaa
wasi`at kulla shay'

Oh Allah, if I was not worthy of reaching Your mercy,
Your mercy is worthy of reaching me because it
encompasses all things.

يَارَبُّ يَارَبُّ يَارَبُّ يَا كَرِيمُ يَا كَرِيمُ يَا كَرِيمُ

Yaa Rabbu! Yaa Rabbu! Yaa Rabb!
Yaa Kareemu! Yaa Kareemu! Yaa Kareem!

Oh Lord! Oh Lord! Oh Lord!
Oh All-generous! Oh All-generous! Oh All-generous!

بِرَحْمَتِكَ يَا أَرْحَمَ الرَّاحِمِيْنَ

Bi-Rahmatika Yaa arhamar-raahimeen
By Your mercy, Oh Most Merciful of the merciful.

أَسْتَغْفِرُ اللَّـهَ (10 مَرَّات)

Astaghfirul-llaah (x 10)
I seek forgiveness from Allah (x 10)

لَا إِلَهَ إِلَّا أَنْتَ سُبْحَانَكَ إِنِّي كُنْتُ مِنَ الظَّالِمِينَ
(3 مَرَّات)

Laa ilaaha illaa anta subhaanaka innee kuntu mi-
na-dh-dhaalimeen (x 3)

There is no god but You, glory be to You, surely I am
one of the transgressors. (x 3)

اللَّهُمَّ إِنِّي أَعُوذُ بِكَ مِنْ نَفْسٍ لاتَشْبَعُ وَمِنْ قَلْبٍ لا
يَخْشَعُ

Allaahumma innee a`oodhu bika min nafsin laa tashba`u
Wa min qalbin laa yakhsha`u

Oh Allah, surely I seek refuge in You from a self which
is
never satiated, And from a heart which is not humble,

وَمِنْ عِلْمٍ لا يَنْفَعُ وَمِنْ صَلاةٍ لا تُرْفَعُ ،وَمِنْ دُعَاءٍ لا
يُسْمَعُ

Wa min `ilmin laa yanfa`u Wa min salaatin laa turfa`u
Wa min du`aa' in laa yusma`u

And from knowledge that does not benefit, And from
prayer that does not reach, And from supplication that
is not heard.

اللَّهُمَّ إِنِّي أَسْأَلُكَ اليُسْرَ بَعْدَ العُسْرِ

Allaahumma innee as'alukal-yusra ba`adal-`usr
Oh Allah, I ask from You ease after difficulty,

وَالفَرَجَ بَعْدَ الكَرْبِ وَالرَّخَاءَ بَعْدَ الشِّدَّةِ

Wal-faraja ba`adal-karb War-rakhaa'a ba`adash-shiddah
And relief after distress, And hope after hardship.

اللَّهُمَّ اجْعَلْ لِي فِي قَلْبِي نُوراً وَبَصَراً وَفَهْماً
وَعِلْمًا إِنَّكَ عَلَى كُلِّ شَيْءٍ قَدِيرٌ

Allaahumma-ja`al lee fee qalbee nooran wa basaran wa fah-man wa`ilman innaka`alaa kulli shay'in qadeer

Oh Allah, put in my heart light and insight and understanding and wisdom. Surely You have power over all things.

لَا إِلَهَ إِلَّا أَنْتَ أَسْتَغْفِرُكَ وَأَتُوبُ إِلَيْكَ

Laa ilaaha illa anta astaghfiruka wa atoobu ilayk

There is no god but You, I seek forgiveness from You & I turn to You.

يَارَبُّ يَارَبُّ يَارَبُّ يَا كَرِيمُ يَا كَرِيمُ يَا كَرِيمُ

Yaa Rabbu! Yaa Rabbu! Yaa Rabb!
Yaa Kareemu! Yaa Kareemu! Yaa Kareem!
Oh Lord! Oh Lord! Oh Lord!
Oh All-generous! Oh All-generous! Oh All-generous!

بِرَحْمَتِكَ يَا أَرْحَمَ الرَّاحِمِينَ

Bi-Rahmatika Yaa arhamar-raahimeen

By Your mercy, Oh Most Merciful of the merciful.

اللَّهُ نَاظِرِى اللَّهُ حَاضِرِى اللَّهُ نَاصِرِى اللَّهُ
حَافِظِى اللَّهُ مَعِى اللَّهُ خَيْرٌ حَافِظًا
(3 مَرَّات)

Allaahu naadhiree. Allaahu haadiree. Allaahu naasiree.
Allaahu haafidhee. Allaahu ma`ee. Allaahu khayrun
haafidhan. (x3)
Allah oversees me. Allah's Presence is upon me.
Allah is my Helper. Allah is my Protector.
Allah is with me. Allah is the best of protectors. (x 3)

أَعُوذُ بِاللَّهِ السَّمِيْعِ العَلِيْمِ مِنَ الشَّيْطَانِ الرَّجِيمِ

A`oodhu billaahis-samee`l-`aleemi minash-shaytaanir-
rajeem
I seek refuge with Allah, the All-hearing, All-seeing,
from the accursed shaytan.

بِسْمِ اللَّهِ الرَّحْمَـٰنِ الرَّحِيمِ

Bismillaahir-rahmaanir-raheem

**In the Name of Allah, the most Beneficent, the most
Merciful.**

يسٓ ۝ وَٱلْقُرْءَانِ ٱلْحَكِيمِ ۝ إِنَّكَ لَمِنَ ٱلْمُرْسَلِينَ ۝
عَلَىٰ صِرَٰطٍ مُّسْتَقِيمٍ ۝ تَنزِيلَ ٱلْعَزِيزِ ٱلرَّحِيمِ ۝ لِتُنذِرَ
قَوْمًا مَّا أُنذِرَ ءَابَآؤُهُمْ فَهُمْ غَـٰفِلُونَ ۝ لَقَدْ حَقَّ ٱلْقَوْلُ
عَلَىٰ أَكْثَرِهِمْ فَهُمْ لَا يُؤْمِنُونَ ۝ إِنَّا جَعَلْنَا فِىٓ أَعْنَـٰقِهِمْ
أَغْلَـٰلًا فَهِىَ إِلَى ٱلْأَذْقَانِ فَهُم مُّقْمَحُونَ ۝ وَجَعَلْنَا مِنۢ
بَيْنِ أَيْدِيهِمْ سَدًّا وَمِنْ خَلْفِهِمْ سَدًّا فَأَغْشَيْنَـٰهُمْ فَهُمْ لَا
يُبْصِرُونَ ۝ وَسَوَآءٌ عَلَيْهِمْ ءَأَنذَرْتَهُمْ أَمْ لَمْ تُنذِرْهُمْ لَا
يُؤْمِنُونَ ۝ إِنَّمَا تُنذِرُ مَنِ ٱتَّبَعَ ٱلذِّكْرَ وَخَشِىَ ٱلرَّحْمَـٰنَ
بِٱلْغَيْبِ فَبَشِّرْهُ بِمَغْفِرَةٍ وَأَجْرٍ كَرِيمٍ ۝

*Yaa-seen. Wal-qur'aanil-hakeem. In-naka la-minal-
mursaleen. `Alaa siraatim mustaqeem. Tanzeelal-`azeezir-
raheem. Li-tundhira qawmam maa undhira aabaa' uhum
fahum ghaa-filoon. Laqad haqqal-qawlu `alaa akthari-him
fahum laa yu'minoon. Innaa ja`alnaa fee a`anaaqihim
aghlaa lan fa-hiya ilal-adhqaani fahum muq-mahoon.
Wa ja`alnaa mim bayni aydeehim saddaw wa min khalfihim
saddan fa-agh shay naahum fahum laa yubsiroon. Wa
sawaa'un `alayhim a-an-dhartahum am lam tundhir-hum
laa yu'minoon. Innamaa tundhiru manit-taba`adh-dhikra
wa khashiyar-rahmaana
Bil-ghayb fa-bash-shirhu bi-maghfira-tin wa ajrin kareem.*
**Ya Seen. By the Qur'an, full of wisdom. You are indeed
one of the messengers, On a straight way. It is sent
down by the Exalted in might, the Most Merciful.**

In order that you may admonish a people whose
fathers had received no admonition, and who
therefore remain heedless. The Word is proved true
against the greater part of them; for they do not
believe. We have put yokes round their necks right up
to their chins, so that their heads are forced up. And
we have put a bar in front of them and a bar behind
them, furthermore We have covered them up so that
they cannot see. It is the same to them whether you
admonish them or not: they will not believe. You can
but admonish such a one as follows The Message and
fears the Lord Most Gracious, unseen; give such a one,
therefore, good tidings of forgiveness and a reward
most generous.

يَٰحَسْرَةً عَلَى ٱلْعِبَادِ مَا يَأْتِيهِم مِّن رَّسُولٍ إِلَّا كَانُوا۟ بِهِۦ
يَسْتَهْزِءُونَ ﴿٣٠﴾

*Yaa hasratan `alal-`ibaadi maa ya'teehim min rasoolin illaa
kaanoo bihi yastah zi'oon.*

Ah alas for (My) servants! There comes not an apostle to
them but they mock him!

وَمَا تَأْتِيهِم مِّنْ ءَايَةٍ مِّنْ ءَايَٰتِ رَبِّهِمْ إِلَّا كَانُوا۟ عَنْهَا
مُعْرِضِينَ ﴿٤٦﴾

*Wa maa ta'teehim min Aayatim min aayaati rabbihim illaa
kaanoo `anhaa mu`rideen*

Not a sign comes to them from among the signs of their
Lord, but they turn away therefrom.

وَيَقُولُونَ مَتَىٰ هَٰذَا ٱلْوَعْدُ إِن كُنتُمْ صَٰدِقِينَ ۝

*Wa ya-qooloona mataa haadhal-wa`adu in kuntum
saadiqeen*

**Furthermore they say, 'When will
this promise (come to pass), if what you say is true!'**

بِسْمِ اللَّهِ الرَّحْمَٰنِ الرَّحِيمِ

Bismil-llaahir-rahmaanir-raheem

In the Name of Allah, the Beneficent, the Merciful

تَبَارَكَ ٱلَّذِى بِيَدِهِ ٱلْمُلْكُ وَهُوَ عَلَىٰ كُلِّ شَىْءٍ قَدِيرٌ ۝
ٱلَّذِى خَلَقَ ٱلْمَوْتَ وَٱلْحَيَوٰةَ لِيَبْلُوَكُمْ أَيُّكُمْ أَحْسَنُ عَمَلًا
وَهُوَ ٱلْعَزِيزُ ٱلْغَفُورُ ۝ ٱلَّذِى خَلَقَ سَبْعَ سَمَٰوَٰتٍ طِبَاقًا
مَّا تَرَىٰ فِى خَلْقِ ٱلرَّحْمَٰنِ مِن تَفَٰوُتٍ فَٱرْجِعِ ٱلْبَصَرَ هَلْ
تَرَىٰ مِن فُطُورٍ ۝ ثُمَّ ٱرْجِعِ ٱلْبَصَرَ كَرَّتَيْنِ يَنقَلِبْ إِلَيْكَ
ٱلْبَصَرُ خَاسِئًا وَهُوَ حَسِيرٌ ۝

*Tabaarakal-ladhee bi-yadihil-mulku wa huwa `alaa kulli
shay'in qadeer Al-ladhee khalaqal-mawta wal-hayaata li-
yabluwakum ayyukum ahsanu `amala wa huwal-`azeezul-
ghafoor Al-ladhee khalaqa saba`a samaawaatin tibaaqam
maa taraa fee khalqir-rahmaani min tafaawutin far ji`il-
basara hal taraa min futoor Thummar ji`il-basara karratayni
yanqalib ilaykal-basaru khaa-si'an wa huwa haseer*

**Blessed be Him in whose hands is dominion; and He
has power over all things; Who created death and life
that He may try which of you is best in deed: and He
is the Exalted in might, Oft-forgiving; Who created
the seven heavens one above another; no want of
proportion can you see in the Creation of (Allah) the
Most Gracious. So turn your vision again: see you any**

flaws? Again turn your vision a second time; (your) vision will come back to you dull and discomfited, in a state worn out.

وَيَقُولُونَ مَتَىٰ هَٰذَا ٱلْوَعْدُ إِن كُنتُمْ صَٰدِقِينَ ﴿٢٥﴾

wa yaquloon mata hadha al wa`d in-kuntum saadeqeen
They say, 'When shall this promise come to pass, if you speak truly?'

سُبْحَانَ رَبِّكَ رَبِّ الْعِزَّةِ عَمَّا يَصِفُونَ وَسَلَامٌ عَلَى الْمُرْسَلِينَ وَالْحَمْدُ لِلهِ رَبِّ الْعَالَمِينَ

Subhaana rabbika rabbil-`izzati `ammaa yasifoon Wa salaamun `alal-mursaleen wal-hamdu lillaahi rabbil-`aalameen
Glory be to your Lord, the Lord of might, above all that they describe, and peace be upon the messengers, and praise belongs to Allah, the Lord of the worlds.

الَّذِينَ قَالَ لَهُمُ النَّاسُ إِنَّ النَّاسَ قَدْ جَمَعُوا لَكُمْ فَاخْشَوْهُمْ فَزَادَهُمْ إِيمَاناً وَقَالُوا: حَسْبُنَا اللهُ وَنِعْمَ الْوَكِيلُ (10 مَرَّات)

Al-ladheena qaala lahu-mun-naasu innan-naasa qad jama`oo lakum fakh shawhum fa-zaadahum eemaanan wa qaaloo Hasbunal-llaahu wa ni`amal-wakeel (x 10)
And the people said to them, 'Men have gathered against you, so fear them.' And it increased them in Iman and they said:
'Allah is enough for us and He is the best guardian.'
(x10)

فَانْقَلَبُوا بِنِعْمَةٍ مِنَ اللَّهِ وَفَضْلٍ لَمْ يَمْسَسْهُمْ سُوءٌ
(3 مَرَّات)

*Fanqalaboo bi-ni'matim minal-llaahi wa fadlil lam yam
sas hum soo' (x 3)*

**So they returned with blessing and fullness from Allah
untouched by evil. (x 3)**

وَاتَّبَعُوا رِضْوَانَ اللَّهِ وَاللَّهُ ذُو فَضْلٍ عَظِيمٍ
(3 مَرَّات)

*Wat-taba'oo ridwaanal-llaah, wal-laahudhu fad-
lin 'adheem (x 3)*

**They followed the good pleasure of Allah, & Allah is of
immense fullness. (x 3)**

وَإِنْ يُرِيدُوا أَنْ يَخْدَعُوكَ فَإِنَّ حَسْبَكَ اللَّهُ هُوَ الَّذِى
أَيَّدَكَ بِنَصْرِهِ وَبِالْمُؤْمِنِينَ وَأَلَّفَ بَيْنَ قُلُوبِهِم لَوْ أَنْفَقْتَ
مَا فِي الْأَرْضِ جَمِيعًا مَا أَلَّفْتَ بَيْنَ قُلُوبِهِم وَلَكِنَّ اللَّهَ
أَلَّفَ بَيْنَهُم إِنَّهُ عَزِيزٌ حَكِيمٌ يَا أَيُّهَا النَّبِيُّ حَسْبُكَ اللَّهُ
وَمَنِ اِتَّبَعَكَ مِنَ الْمُؤْمِنِينَ
(3 مَرَّات)

*Wa in yureedoo an yakh da'ooka fa-inna has bakal-llaah
Huwal-ladhee ay-yadaka bi-nasreehee Wa bil-mu'mineen Wa
al-lafa bayna quloobihim, Lao anfaq-ta maa fil-ardi jamee'an
maa al-lafta bayna quloobihim, Wa laakinnal-llaaha al-lafa
baynahum, innahu 'azeezun hakeem, Yaa ayyuhan-nabeeyyu
hasbukal-llaahu wa manit-taba'aka min al-mu'mineen (x 3)*

**And if they desire to trick you, Allah is enough for you.
He has confirmed you with His help, and the trusting
ones and has brought their hearts together. Had you**

expended all that is in the earth, you could not have
brought their hearts together, but Allah brought their
hearts together. He is Mighty, and Wise. Oh Prophet,
Allah is enough for you, and the trusting ones who
follow you. (x 3)

بِسْمِ اللَّهِ الرَّحْمَٰنِ الرَّحِيمِ

Bismil-llaahir-rahmaanir-raheem
In the name of Allah, the Beneficent, the Merciful,

قُلْ هُوَ ٱللَّهُ أَحَدٌ ۝ ٱللَّهُ ٱلصَّمَدُ ۝ لَمْ يَلِدْ وَلَمْ يُولَدْ ۝
وَلَمْ يَكُن لَّهُۥ كُفُوًا أَحَدٌ ۝

*Qul huwal-llaahu ahad Allaahus-samad Lam yalid wa lam
yoolad Wa lam yakul lahu kufuwan ahad*
Say: He, Allah is One, Allah is Eternal, He begets not,
nor is He begotten, And there is nothing equal unto
Him.

بِسْمِ اللَّهِ الرَّحْمَٰنِ الرَّحِيمِ

Bismil-llaahir-rahmaanir-raheem
In the name of Allah, the Beneficent, the Merciful,

قُلْ يَٰٓأَيُّهَا ٱلْكَٰفِرُونَ ۝ لَآ أَعْبُدُ مَا تَعْبُدُونَ ۝ وَلَآ أَنتُمْ عَٰبِدُونَ مَآ أَعْبُدُ ۝ وَلَآ أَنَا۠ عَابِدٌ مَّا عَبَدتُّمْ ۝ وَلَآ أَنتُمْ عَٰبِدُونَ مَآ أَعْبُدُ ۝ لَكُمْ دِينُكُمْ وَلِيَ دِينِ ۝

Qul yaa ayyuhal-kaafiroon Laa `abudu maa t`abudoon
Wa laa antum `aabidoona maa a`bud Wa laa ana `aabidun
maa `abad-tum Wa laa antum `aabidoona maa a`bud Lakum
deenukum wa liya deen
Say: Oh you who do not believe! I do not worship what
you worship, Nor do you worship what I worship, Nor
will I worship what you worship, Nor will you worship
what I worship. You shall have your path and I shall
have my path.

بِسْمِ اللَّهِ الرَّحْمَٰنِ الرَّحِيمِ

Bismil-llaahir-rahmaanir-raheem
In the name of Allah, the Beneficent, the Merciful,

قُلْ أَعُوذُ بِرَبِّ ٱلْفَلَقِ ۝ مِن شَرِّ مَا خَلَقَ ۝ وَمِن شَرِّ غَاسِقٍ إِذَا وَقَبَ ۝ وَمِن شَرِّ ٱلنَّفَّٰثَٰتِ فِى ٱلْعُقَدِ ۝ وَمِن شَرِّ حَاسِدٍ إِذَا حَسَدَ ۝

Qul a`oodhu bi-rabbil-falaq Min sharri maa khalaq Wa min
shar-ri ghaasiqin idha waqab Wa min shar-rin-naf faa thaa-ti
fil-`uqad Wa min sharri haasidin idha hasad
Say: I seek refuge in the Lord of the dawn, From the
evil of what He has created, And from the evil of the
dark night when it comes, And from the evil of those

who blow on knots, And from the evil of the envious
when he envies.

بِسْمِ اللَّـهِ الرَّحْمَـٰنِ الرَّحِيمِ

Bismil-llaahir-rahmaanir-raheem
In the Name of Allah, the Beneficent, the Merciful,

قُلْ أَعُوذُ بِرَبِّ ٱلنَّاسِ ۞ مَلِكِ ٱلنَّاسِ ۞ إِلَٰهِ ٱلنَّاسِ ۞
مِن شَرِّ ٱلْوَسْوَاسِ ٱلْخَنَّاسِ ۞ ٱلَّذِى يُوَسْوِسُ فِى صُدُورِ
ٱلنَّاسِ ۞ مِنَ ٱلْجِنَّةِ وَٱلنَّاسِ ۞

Qul a`oodhu bi-rabbin-naas Malikin-naas Ilaahin-naas
Min sharril-waswaasil-khan-naas Al-ladhee yuwaswisu fee
sudoorin-naas Minal-jinnati wan-naas
Say: I seek refuge in the Lord of men, The King of men,
The God of men, From the evil whisperings of the
slinking shaytan, who whispers into the hearts of men,
From among the jinn and the men.

لَا إِلَهَ إِلَّا اللَّـهُ   (14 مَرَّة)

Laa ilaa ha illal-llaah (x 14)
There is no god but Allah (x 14)